Contents

Meet the Tyrannosaurus rex

The Tyrannosaurus rex was

a dinosaur that ate meat.

It hunted many other

species of dinosaur.

Pebble® Plus

DINOSAURS

TYRANNOSAURUS REX

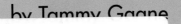

by Tammy Gagne

Raintree is an imprint of Capstone Global Library Limited, a company incorporated in England and Wales having its registered office at 264 Banbury Road, Oxford, OX2 7DY – Registered company number: 6695582

www.raintree.co.uk
myorders@raintree.co.uk

Edited by Hank Musolf
Designed by Charmaine Whitman
Picture research by Kelly Garvin
Production by Laura Manthe
Illustrated by Jon Hughes/Capstone Press
Originated by Capstone Global Library Ltd
Printed and bound in India

ISBN 978 1 4747 5221 3 (hardback)
22 21 20 19 18
10 9 8 7 6 5 4 3 2 1

ISBN 978 1 4747 5227 5 (paperback)
23 22 21 20 19
10 9 8 7 6 5 4 3 2 1

British Library Cataloguing in Publication Data
A full catalogue record for this book is available from the British Library.

Design elements: Shutterstock/Krasovski Dmitri

Every effort has been made to contact copyright holders of material reproduced in this book. Any omissions will be rectified in subsequent printings if notice is given to the publisher.

All the internet addresses (URLs) given in this book were valid at the time of going to press. However, due to the dynamic nature of the internet, some addresses may have changed, or sites may have changed or ceased to exist since publication. While the author and publisher regret any inconvenience this may cause readers, no responsibility for any such changes can be accepted by either the author or the publisher.

An adult Tyrannosaurus rex was up to 6 metres (20 feet) tall. It weighed about 8 tonnes!

The Tyrannosaurus rex had a large head and tail. Its strong back legs helped it to run up to 40 kilometres (25 miles) per hour. But its short front legs could not reach its mouth.

Bone crushers

The Tyrannosaurus rex was a carnivore. It hunted other dinosaurs. It could eat 230 kilograms (500 pounds) of meat in one bite!

The teeth of the Tyrannosaurus rex were cone shaped. These teeth could grab and bite prey. Strong jaws crushed bones.

What big feet they had

The Tyrannosaurus rex lived
about 70 million years ago.
It lived in North America.
Scientists think the
Tyrannosaurus rex moved to
different places.

Scientists have found bones from a

Tyrannosaurus rex in Montana,

USA. A Tyrannosaurus rex

footprint was found in

New Mexico, USA. It was

86 centimetres (34 inches) long!

Working together

The Tyrannosaurus rex had

a large brain.

This species of dinosaur

was clever.

Scientists think this species hunted in packs. The fast, young dinosaurs chased prey. The slower adults killed the prey when they caught up.

Glossary

carnivore animal that eats meat

prey animal that is hunted by another animal

scientist person who studies the way the world works

species group of animals with similar features

Read more

Dinosaurs: a children's encyclopedia,
DK (DK Children, 2011)

A Weekend with Dinosaurs (Fantasy Field Trips),
Claire Throp (Raintree, 2015)

World's Scariest Dinosaurs (Extreme Dinosaurs),
Rupert Matthews (Raintree, 2012)

Websites

www.bbc.co.uk/cbeebies/curations/dinosaur-facts

www.dkfindout.com/uk/dinosaurs-and-prehistoric-life/
dinosaurs/tyrannosaurus/

Comprehension questions

1. How did Tyrannosaurus rex feed itself if its front legs couldn't reach its mouth?

2. How do you think the shape of the Tyrannosaurus rex's teeth helped it in hunting?

3. How might scientists learn from fossils that Tyrannosaurus rex lived in groups?

Index